It's all about…

EXOTIC
EGYPTIANS

KINGFISHER

⚲ KINGFISHER

First published 2017 by Kingfisher
An imprint of Macmillan Children's Books
20 New Wharf Road, London N1 9RR
Associated companies throughout the world
www.panmacmillan.com

Series editor: Sarah Snashall
Series design: Anthony Hannant (LittleRedAnt)
Adapted from an original text by Philip Steele

ISBN 978-0-7534-3934-0

9 8 7 6 5 4 3 2 1

1TR/0716/WKT/UG/128MA

A CIP catalogue record for this book is available from the British Library.

Printed in China

Picture credits
The Publisher would like to thank the following for permission to reproduce their material.
Top = t; Bottom = b; Centre = c; Left = l; Right = r
Front cover iStock/tepic; back cover Shutterstock/Vladimir Wrangel; Pages 1 iStock/tepic;
2–3, 30–31 iStock/Berthold Engelmann; 4 iStock/dogayusufdokdok; 5 iStock/Terraxplorer;
6 iStock/oversnap; 7 Kingfisher Artbank; 7c iStock/alexerich; 8–9 Kingfisher Artbank;
8t Art Archive/DEA picture library; 9t iStock/majaiva; 10 Kingfisher Artbank;
11 Shutterstock/Styve Reineck; 12–13 iStock/karimhesham; 13 Alamy/Carolyn Clarke;
14 Shutterstock/Pecold; 15t Alamy/Jose Lucas; 15b Alamy/epa european pressphoto
agency; 16 Alamy/Lanmas; 17c Walters Art Museum; 17b Alamy/Steve Vidler; 18 iStock/
hanoded; 19t Edwin Smythe 19b Shutterstock/AISA-Everett; 20 Alamy/Robert Harding;
21t Alamy/Art Archive; 21b Getty/Leemage; 22 Einsamer Schütze; 23t Alamy/Robert
Harding; 23b, 24 Alamy/The Print Collector; 25t Guillame Blanchard; 25bg iStock/
TerryJLawrence; 25b Shutterstock/Vladimir Wrangel; 26, 27b, 28 Alamy/Heritage Image
Partnerships Ltd; 27t Getty/DEA/G Lovera; 29 Alamy/Art Archive.
Cards Front tl iStock/Ugurhan Betin; tr Neues Museum; bl Shutterstock/Jaroslav Moravcik;
Back tl Art Archive/DeA Picture Library/S Vannini; tr Shutterstock/mountainpix; bl Alamy/
National Geographic Creative; br Alamy/Jose Lucas.

You will find c. before some dates. This stands for *circa*, which means 'about'.

Front cover: The gold death mask of the boy-king Tutankhamun.

CONTENTS

For your free audio download go to
http://panmacmillan.com/exoticegyptians
or goo.gl/8eDyxz
Happy listening!

The Ancient Egyptians

In 3100 BCE (about 5000 years ago) Upper and Lower Egypt became one country under a king named Narmer. The time of the pharaohs had begun. It lasted for 3000 years until Egypt became part of the Roman Empire in 31 BCE.

The Great Sphinx statue has the body of a lion and the face of a king.

The Ancient Egyptians are famous for their huge temples and pyramids, their exotic pharaohs, colourful wall paintings, animal-headed gods and strange hieroglyphics.

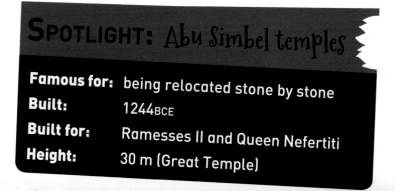

SPOTLIGHT: Abu Simbel temples

Famous for: being relocated stone by stone
Built: 1244BCE
Built for: Ramesses II and Queen Nefertiti
Height: 30 m (Great Temple)

The mighty Nile

If you fly over Egypt in a plane, you can see great sandy deserts below. Only a narrow green strip marks the course of the River Nile.

In ancient times, the Nile flooded every summer. The floods made the soil very fertile for growing crops, and so farmers first settled along the banks of the river. The Nile also provided water to drink and to irrigate the fields.

SPOTLIGHT: River Nile

Famous for: central to Egyptian life
Gave farms: water and rich soil
Gave cities: trade, papyrus, transport, bricks
Wildlife: crocodile, fish, heron, hippo, ibis

Mediterranean Sea

Delta

Lower Egypt

Giza

Memphis

River Nile

The Egyptians made boats from reeds or wood to travel on the river.

Upper Egypt

Thebes

The Nile flows north into the Mediterranean Sea.

The kingdom of Egypt

Ancient Egypt was ruled by a pharaoh. The pharaoh was an all-powerful ruler and was treated almost like a god. All other Egyptians had their place in society beneath the pharaoh.

This mortuary temple was built by Queen Hatshepsut.

FACT...

Pharaoh

There were a few female pharaohs, including Hatshepsut and Cleopatra.

Royal family, leading priests, officials and army commanders

Doctors, engineers, traders, scribes and architects

Minor priests and craft workers

Soldiers, sailors, servants and performers

Labourers and slaves

Gods and goddesses

There were at least 740 Egyptian gods and goddesses. Painters showed the gods with horns or a beak, or the head of an animal.

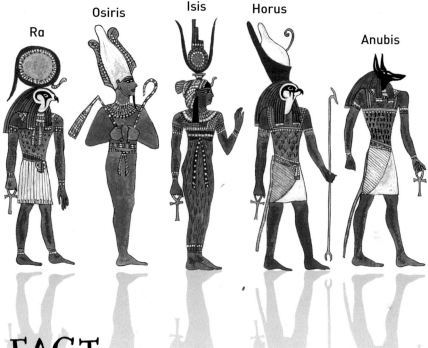

Ra

Osiris

Isis

Horus

Anubis

FACT...

The pharaoh Akhenaten believed there was just one god, called Aten. His son, Tutankhamun, went back to worshipping lots of different gods.

Ra was the sun god; Anubis the god for mummies. Osiris was the god of the dead and his wife Isis was the mother goddess. Horus protected Egypt and its rulers.

The pharaohs belonged to the family of the gods. If the pharaohs did not do their duty, then the whole world would fall apart.

The Ancient Egyptians built temples to their gods, where priests made offerings.

The pyramids

Between June and September every year, the Nile flooded the fields. Labourers could not work on the land, so instead they would join the thousands of workers building temples or monuments, such as pyramids.

SPOTLIGHT: Great Pyramid of Giza

Famous for:	tallest building for 3800 years
Built for:	King Khufu
Built from:	2.3 million stone blocks
Height:	139 m

the pyramids at Giza, near Cairo

Pyramids were the tombs of pharaohs. Inside were secret chambers filled with treasures that the pharaoh could use in the next world.

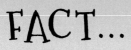

FACT...

Pharaohs would start planning for their burial as soon as they became ruler.

The tombs of the pharaohs had painted walls and ceilings.

Tutankhamun's treasures

Tomb robbers soon learned that the pyramids were full of gold, so pharaohs started to build their tombs in a secret valley. Archaeologists have found 63 burial places here. The best-preserved one is the tomb of Tutankhamun.

The secret valley is now called the Valley of the Kings.

SPOTLIGHT: Tomb of Tutankhamun

Famous for:	treasure-filled tomb
Where:	Valley of the Kings
Sealed:	1323 BCE
Opened:	1922 (by Howard Carter)

Tutankhamun's death mask is made of solid gold decorated with gemstones and coloured glass.

FACT...

Tutankhamun was buried with chariot wheels, trumpets, food, daggers, golden thrones, wooden animals, boats, golden sandals and much more.

Tutankhamun's tomb was filled with luxury objects for him to use in the world of the dead.

Making mummies

The wealthiest Egyptians wanted one more thing preserved in their tomb – their carefully prepared body.

First, the priests cleaned the body. They pulled the brain out through the nose and cut out the guts, liver and lungs.

The mummy was placed in a casket.

The body was dried for 40 days in a special kind of salt, and then stuffed with cloth or sawdust. Finally it was covered in resin and oil and wrapped in linen bandages.

The brain, guts, liver and lungs were placed in four separate canopic jars, such as these.

FACT...

Egyptians made mummies of cats to honour the cat goddess, Bastet.

17

Ways of writing

Egyptian priests wrote using a system of pictures and shapes called hieroglyphics. Each symbol (or hieroglyph) stood for a sound, an idea or an object. Professional writers called scribes would write documents or letters in a quicker script.

The Egyptians wrote on paper made from papyrus reeds. They carved their hieroglyphs on temples and many other monuments.

Letters and documents were written on papyrus using reed pens or brushes and black or red ink.

FACT...

The word papyrus gives us our modern word 'paper'.

Hieroglyphs provided decoration as well as information.

The farmer's year

Most Egyptians lived in villages along the banks of the Nile. Farmers dug channels to bring water from the river through their fields.

Every November, farmers planted wheat and barley for harvest in the spring. They also grew peas, beans, cabbages, leeks, cucumbers, dates, figs, grapes and melons.

Oxen pulled the farmer's plough.

During the summer floods, the farmers would mend their tools or work on building projects for the pharaoh.

FACT...

In some areas, hippopotamuses came out of the river at night and trampled over the crops on the banks.

Women made bread or beer from the grain.

A child's life

Children played with rattles, balls, spinning tops and toy lions and crocodiles. They wrestled and swam in the Nile. But most children had to work when they were quite small. Girls learned how to weave cloth and cook. Children from important families, especially boys, learned reading, writing and sums.

This carved horse would have been pulled along by a string.

Boys helped in the fields, or worked in their father's workshop.

FACT...

Children in Ancient Egypt often wore no clothes and ran around naked.

Boys shaved off their hair, apart from a side lock.

Clothes and jewels

The Egyptians wore light, loose clothes. Women wore long dresses; men wore a tunic or just a length of cloth worn around the waist like a skirt. Their clothes were sometimes decorated with pleats or folds. Poor people wore sandals made from papyrus or grass; rich people wore leather sandals.

Nobles wore wigs decorated with beads and ribbons. They also wore broad collars made of beads.

Egyptian jewellery
was made of gold and
semi-precious stones.

FACT...

At important events
the pharaoh wore a false
beard – even the female
pharaohs did this!

Kings and queens,
such as Nefertiti shown
here, wore elaborate
headdresses.

Traders and explorers

The Egyptians did not use money or metal coins. They exchanged goods or services with a system called bartering. In the market they would swap grain for pots and jars, or a piece of jewellery for a knife.

The Egyptians weighed goods ready to barter them.

Egyptian explorers sailed down the Red Sea. They brought back ivory, precious woods, incense and wild animals such as pet monkeys and sacred baboons.

The Egyptians sailed around the Mediterranean Sea and Arabia to trade.

FACT...

Traders brought the blue stone lapis lazuli 4000 kilometres from Afghanistan to Egypt.

Egypt at war

The Egyptians believed that their pharaohs should rule all the lands created by the gods. Pictures show the pharaohs crushing Egypt's enemies.

Soldiers fought with bows and arrows, swords, axes and spears, and carried shields and clubs called maces. They hurled stones at their enemies with slings.

Some pharaohs were buried with armies of lifelike model soldiers.

This ceremonial knife has a carved ivory handle and a flint blade.

Famous for: greatest battle of Ancient Egypt

What: war between Egyptians and Hittites

When: 1288BCE

Where: Qadesh, Syria

Ramesses II fought from his war chariot.

GLOSSARY

archaeologist A person who finds and studies remains and ruins from long ago.

architect A person who designs buildings.

barter To swap one thing for another, instead of using money.

BCE Short for 'Before the Common Era' (any date before 1CE). It is also sometimes known as BC (before Christ).

delta A coastal area where a build-up of mud forces a river to split into separate streams.

fertile Good for growing strong, healthy crops.

hieroglyphics System of picture writing used in Ancient Egypt.

incense Wood or gum that smells sweet when burned.

irrigate To put water onto something (usually crops).

ivory A hard material made from elephants' tusks.

lapis lazuli A bright-blue precious stone.

mace A weapon like a heavy club.

mummy A dead body that has been dried and prepared so it does not rot.

offering Food or drink, or another gift presented to a god or goddess.

papyrus A thick kind of paper made from the reeds of the papyrus plant.

pharaoh A king or queen of Ancient Egypt.

pyramid A stone monument with a square base and triangular sides.

resin A thick, sticky liquid that comes mainly from trees.

scribe Someone whose job is to copy writing or make notes; an official in Ancient Egypt.

sphinx A statue with the body of a lion and the head of a human.

INDEX

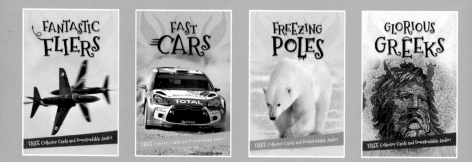
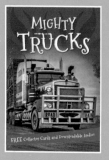

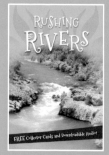